ADORNING THE D.

MW00905688

THE POETRY OF STEPHEN D. RHOADES

ENHANCED BY THE BREATHTAKING RIYA ALBERT

Printed in the United States of America

First Printing 2020

ISBN: 9798583149179

Imprint: Independently published

INTRODUCTION

"While it may sound cliché', I truly am humbled by this opportunity to be allowed to use the stunning photos of Riya Albert in this book. For a while I have seen her photos shared on social media and was always amazed on how the genius of the photographer was evident in how they captured so much in every image. I was equally struck by how Riya Albert conveyed so much through her eyes, and various expressions. When I write, I am writing about what many people miss in others and putting words to what many cannot. I am inspired by what the eyes, facial expressions, and body language says about a person. With Riya Albert, she fit perfectly with many poems I had written in the past. One of the coolest things is that I write on a wide range of topics and her, along with her photographer, managed to capture all those in different ways. Which is incredible in itself. So when I approached Riya about using her pictures in a book along with my poetry, she made my day by saying yes. So here it is. I'm absolutely thrilled by how it turned out and hope you enjoy it as much as I have enjoyed putting it together."

Stephen D. Rhoades
(S.D.R.)
Shakespeare's Raven 2

'To simply say you're beautiful is not completely true. That is only because there is not an adjective for beauty that can accurately describe you. Perhaps among the whispers of angel's such beauty has been spoken of. Maybe I have come close when I attempt to describe the heavens above. Otherwise there isn't a word for beauty that will ever do when I try to accurately describe you."

Stephen D. Rhoades

(S.D.R.)

Shakespeare's Raven 2

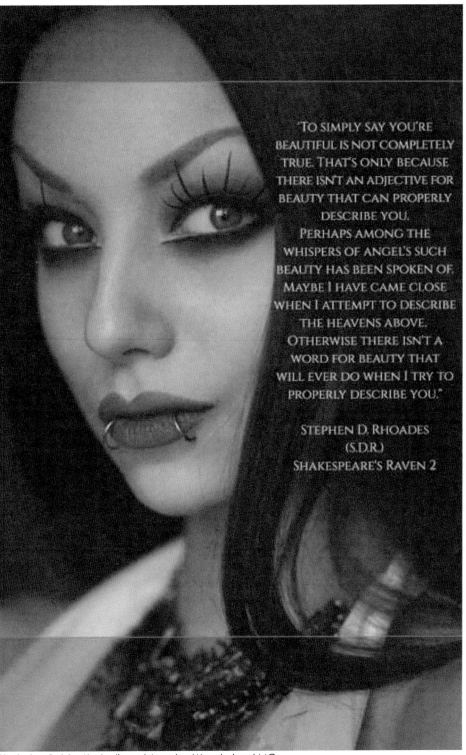

"TO SIMPLY SAY YOU'RE
BEAUTIFUL IS NOT COMPLETELY
TRUE. THAT'S ONLY BECAUSE
THERE ISN'T AN ADJECTIVE FOR
BEAUTY THAT CAN PROPERLY
DESCRIBE YOU.
PERHAPS AMONG THE
WHISPERS OF ANGEL'S SUCH
BEAUTY HAS BEEN SPOKEN OF.
MAYBE I HAVE CAME CLOSE
WHEN I ATTEMPT TO DESCRIBE
THE HEAVENS ABOVE.
OTHERWISE THERE ISN'T A
WORD FOR BEAUTY THAT
WILL EVER DO WHEN I TRY TO
PROPERLY DESCRIBE YOU."

STEPHEN D. RHOADES
(S.D.R.)
SHAKESPEARE'S RAVEN 2

Photo by: Bobby Kostadinov / Jewelry: Wonderland MC

"My sins need holy water but the sweat from your body will do. I am about to confess a very specific sin to you. Not with words but in deed. I will show you how demon's breed."

Stephen D. Rhoades

(S.D.R.)

Shakespeare's Raven 2

"MY SINS NEED HOLY WATER BUT THE SWEAT FROM YOUR BODY
WILL DO. I'M ABOUT TO CONFESS A VERY SPECIFIC SIN TO YOU.
NOT WITH WORDS BUT IN DEED. I WILL SHOW YOU HOW DEMON'S
BREED."

STEPHEN D. RHOADES
(S.D.R.)
SHAKESPEARE'S RAVEN 2

Photo: Riya Albert / Clothing & Accessories: KIllstart

"She is the poetry that I'm unable to properly write.

She is the music that soothes my soul amid a sleepless night."

Stephen D. Rhoades

(S.D.R.)

Shakespeare's Raven 2

"She is the poetry that I'm unable to properly write.
She is the the music that soothes my soul amid a sleepless night."

Stephen D. Rhoades

(S.D.R.)

Shakespeare's Raven 2

Photo by: Riya Albert / Clothing: Dark in love

"Her broken pieces took on wings.

Her strong voice was something only an angel sings.

An abstract beauty born out of pain.

Their violence, and cruelty, became her gain.

Her rise from the ashes proved nothing was in vain.

From ugliness that others threw her way, she became the dawn of a brand-new day.

From darkness into the light, she refused to stay down and got up to fight.

With determination and a heart of gold, she refused to believe the lies she had been told.

Rising with the morning sun, she proved she was not done.

Stephen D. Rhoades

(S.D.R.)

Shakespeare's Raven 2

"HER BROKEN PIECES TOOK ON WINGS.
HER STRONG VOICE WAS SOMETHING ONLY AN ANGEL SINGS.
AN ABSTRACT BEAUTY BORN OUT OF PAIN.
THEIR VIOLENCE, AND CRUELTY BECAME HER GAIN.
HER RISE FROM THE ASHES PROVED NOTHING WAS IN VAIN.
FROM UGLINESS THAT OTHERS THREW HER WAY, SHE BECAME THE
DAWN OF A BRAND NEW DAY.
FROM DARKNESS INTO THE LIGHT, SHE REFUSED TO STAY DOWN
AND GOT UP TO FIGHT.
WITH DETERMINATION AND A HEART OF GOLD, SHE REFUSED TO
BELIEVE THE LIES SHE HAD BEEN TOLD.
RISING WITH THE MORNING SUN, SHE PROVED SHE WASN'T DONE.

STEPHEN D. RHOADES
(S.D.R.)
SHAKESPEARE'S RAVEN 2

"Speak to me of angels and will tell you that I heard one sing. Tell me of beauty and I will tell you of one that is beyond amazing. Ask me if I believe in heaven and I will simply point to her. Then I will reply, "How can I not with the way she makes my heart stir?"

Paint me a picture of the stars and radiant moon beams. I will draw with words a woman in which every man dreams.

Write to me about strength, beauty, intelligence, and love.

I will write back to you about an angel sent from up above."

Stephen D. Rhoades

(S.D.R.)

Shakespeare's Raven 2

"SPEAK TO ME OF ANGELS AND WILL TELL YOU THAT I HEARD ONE SING. TELL ME OF
BEAUTY AND I WILL TELL YOU OF ONE THAT IS BEYOND AMAZING. ASK ME IF I BELIEVE
IN HEAVEN AND I WILL SIMPLY POINT TO HER. THEN I WILL REPLY, "HOW CAN I NOT
WITH THE WAY SHE MAKES MY HEART STIR?"

PAINT ME A PICTURE OF THE STARS AND RADIANT MOON BEAMS. I WILL DRAW WITH
WORDS A WOMAN IN WHICH EVERY MAN DREAMS.

WRITE TO ME ABOUT ABOUT STRENGTH, BEAUTY, INTELLIGENCE, AND LOVE.

I WILL WRITE BACK TO YOU ABOUT AN ANGEL SENT FROM UP ABOVE."

STEPHEN D. RHOADES
(S.D.R.)
SHAKESPEARE'S RAVEN 2

Photo by : Riva Albert

"I saw the fire in her eyes despite the tears that fell like rain. I also noticed strength that accompanied the pain. I heard the words she could not express. Above all, I saw the beauty in everything she considered a mess."

Stephen D. Rhoades

(S.D.R.)

Shakespeare's Raven 2

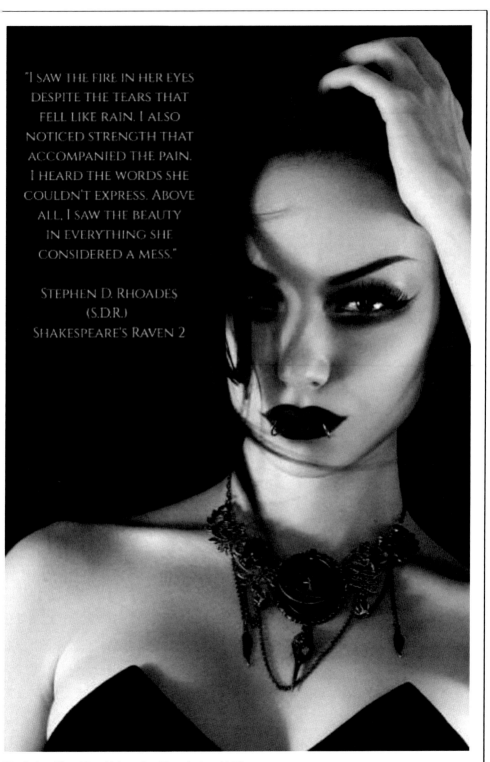

"I SAW THE FIRE IN HER EYES
DESPITE THE TEARS THAT
FELL LIKE RAIN. I ALSO
NOTICED STRENGTH THAT
ACCOMPANIED THE PAIN.
I HEARD THE WORDS SHE
COULDN'T EXPRESS. ABOVE
ALL, I SAW THE BEAUTY
IN EVERYTHING SHE
CONSIDERED A MESS."

STEPHEN D. RHOADES
(S.D.R.)
SHAKESPEARE'S RAVEN 2

Photo by: Riya Albert/ Jewelry: Wonderland MC

"She is the definition of beauty that I have spent my life trying to describe in detail.

Beauty I have tried to capture, but each adjective seemed to fail. This is beauty that every man dreams of. This is beauty that Angels describe in hushed whispers while peering down from up above."

Stephen D. Rhoades

(S.D.R.)

Shakespeare's Raven 2

"SHE IS THE DEFINITION OF BEAUTY THAT I HAVE SPENT MY LIFE TRYING TO DESCRIBE IN DETAIL. BEAUTY I HAVE TRIED TO CAPTURE, BUT EACH ADJECTIVE SEEMED TO FAIL. THIS IS BEAUTY THAT EVERY MAN DREAMS OF. THIS IS BEAUTY THAT ANGELS DESCRIBE IN HUSHED WHISPERS WHILE PEERING DOWN FROM UP ABOVE."

STEPHEN D. RHOADES
(S.D.R.)
SHAKESPEARE'S RAVEN 2

Photo by: Veni Georgiev / Clothing: Killstar

"She was a book that so many never read. They admired the cover but were clueless on what the pages said. She gave me the right to see what had previously been forbidden. She let me read every word that had been written. Next, she gave me the privilege of seeing her naked while she was still fully clothed. I was given the gift of her trusting me as she allowed her soul to be exposed.

Then, and only then, was I allowed to touch her skin."

Stephen D. Rhoades

(S.D.R.)

Shakespeare's Raven 2

"SHE WAS A BOOK THAT SO MANY NEVER READ. THEY ADMIRED THE COVER, BUT WERE CLUELESS ON WHAT THE PAGES SAID. SHE GAVE ME THE RIGHT TO SEE WHAT HAD PREVIOUSLY BEEN FORBIDDEN. SHE LET ME READ EVERY WORD THAT HAD BEEN WRITTEN. NEXT SHE GAVE ME THE PRIVILEGE OF SEEING HER NAKED WHILE SHE WAS STILL FULLY CLOTHED. I WAS GIVEN THE GIFT OF HER TRUSTING ME AS SHE ALLOWED HER SOUL TO BE EXPOSED. THEN, AND ONLY THEN, WAS I ALLOWED TO TOUCH HER SKIN."

STEPHEN D. RHOADES
(S.D.R.)

Photo by: Bobby Kostadinov / Clothing and accessories: Killstar

"Much like the intensity of the vampires kiss, so is the darkest and deepest moments of secret erotic bliss. The soft but firm touches of hands against skin. My drug of choice and favorite sin. Where words are seldom needed while the primal desires are heeded. Tracing what I want to do to you in the sweat that forms on your skin. Using my lips to repeat it again and again. One last ravenous kiss before you go. Some of the best secrets are ones no one else will ever know."

Stephen D. Rhoades

(S.D.R.)

Shakespeare's Raven 2

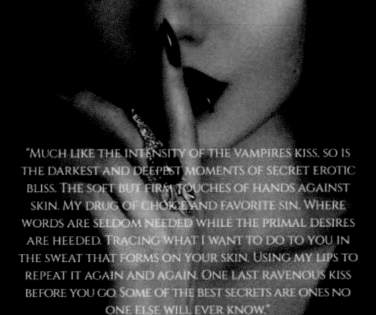

"MUCH LIKE THE INTENSITY OF THE VAMPIRES KISS, SO IS
THE DARKEST AND DEEPEST MOMENTS OF SECRET EROTIC
BLISS. THE SOFT BUT FIRM TOUCHES OF HANDS AGAINST
SKIN. MY DRUG OF CHOICE AND FAVORITE SIN. WHERE
WORDS ARE SELDOM NEEDED WHILE THE PRIMAL DESIRES
ARE HEEDED. TRACING WHAT I WANT TO DO TO YOU IN
THE SWEAT THAT FORMS ON YOUR SKIN. USING MY LIPS TO
REPEAT IT AGAIN AND AGAIN. ONE LAST RAVENOUS KISS
BEFORE YOU GO. SOME OF THE BEST SECRETS ARE ONES NO
ONE ELSE WILL EVER KNOW."

STEPHEN D. RHOADES
(S.D.R.)
SHAKESPEARE'S RAVEN 2

Photo by: Riva Albert / Jewelry: Mystic Thread

"Listen, I'm simply going to love the hell out of you as we suffocate on each other's kiss while breathing in each other's soul.

I will make love to you and break the damn bed while making you feel whole. I will take your heart and sew it to mine and it will beat as one, and if I'm able, I will still be with you when time on this Earth is done."

Got it?

Stephen D. Rhoades

(S.D.R.)

Shakespeare's Raven 2

"LISTEN, I'M SIMPLY GOING TO LOVE THE HELL
OUT OF YOU AS WE SUFFOCATE ON EACH
OTHER'S KISS WHILE BREATHING IN EACH
OTHER'S SOUL.
I WILL MAKE LOVE TO YOU AND BREAK THE
DAMN BED WHILE MAKING YOU FEEL WHOLE.
I WILL TAKE YOUR HEART AND SEW IT TO MINE
AND IT WILL BEAT AS ONE. AND IF I'M ABLE, I
WILL STILL BE WITH YOU WHEN TIME ON THIS
EARTH IS DONE."
GOT IT?

STEPHEN D. RHOADES
(S.D.R.)
SHAKESPEARE'S RAVEN 2

Photo by: Veni Georgiev / Accessories: Mystic Thread

"There was a fierceness in her beauty in the way I could see her soul in her eyes.

They glowed with a flame that flickers, but never dies."

Stephen D. Rhoades

(S.D.R.)

Shakespeare's Raven 2

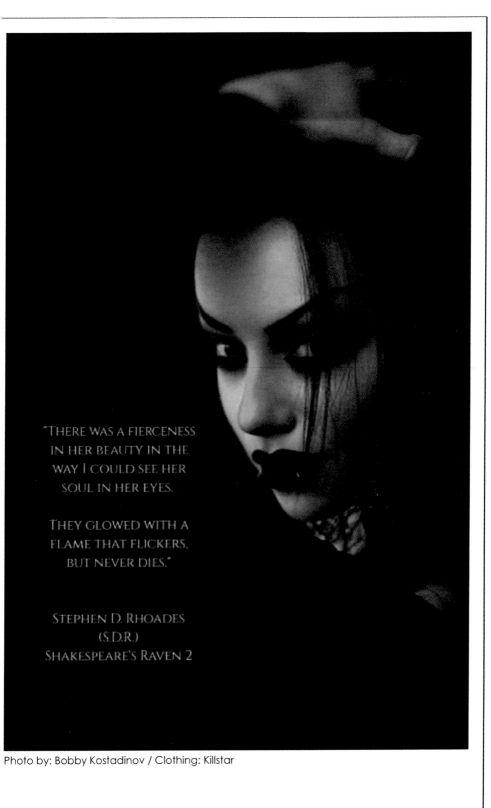

"THERE WAS A FIERCENESS
IN HER BEAUTY IN THE
WAY I COULD SEE HER
SOUL IN HER EYES.

THEY GLOWED WITH A
FLAME THAT FLICKERS,
BUT NEVER DIES."

STEPHEN D. RHOADES
(S.D.R.)
SHAKESPEARE'S RAVEN 2

Photo by: Bobby Kostadinov / Clothing: Killstar

"When you write about her, her eyes are the place to start. Pay close attention and you will soon see her heart. You will see both the good and the bad. You will sense what brings her joy, and what makes her sad. Never stop searching her eyes. For behind them is where the truth lies."

Stephen D. Rhoades

(S.D.R.)

Shakespeare's Raven 2

"WHEN YOU WRITE ABOUT HER, HER EYES ARE THE PLACE TO START. PAY CLOSE ATTENTION AND YOU WILL SOON SEE HER HEART. YOU'LL SEE BOTH THE GOOD AND THE BAD. YOU WILL SENSE WHAT BRINGS HER JOY, AND WHAT MAKES HER SAD. NEVER STOP SEARCHING HER EYES. FOR BEHIND THEM IS WHERE THE TRUTH LIES."

STEPHEN D. RHOADES
(S.D.R.)
SHAKESPEARE'S RAVEN 2

Photo by: Bobby Kostadinov / Clothing: Killstar

"She takes the pain and makes music with it that is worded by every scar."

The world's most beautiful symphony, where she is both the conductor and the star."

Stephen D. Rhoades

(S.D.R.)

Shakespeare's Raven 2

"SHE TAKES THE PAIN AND MAKES MUSIC WITH IT THAT IS
WORDED BY EVERY SCAR."
THE WORLD'S MOST BEAUTIFUL SYMPHONY, WHERE SHE IS
BOTH THE CONDUCTOR AND THE STAR."

STEPHEN D. RHOADES
(S.D.R.)
SHAKESPEARE'S RAVEN 2

"It's a whisper of a lonely heart I hear when I stand close to you. I sense a longing for a love that is long overdue. Your eyes tell a story of such a heartbreaking tale. Sorted chapters of both regret and heartless betrayal. I see the searching and the hope that flickers like a candle barely burning. I see the tears being held back as you stay quiet while silently yearning."

Stephen D. Rhoades

(S.D.R.)

Shakespeare's Raven 2

"IT'S A WHISPER OF A LONELY HEART I HEAR WHEN I STAND
CLOSE TO YOU. I SENSE A LONGING FOR A LOVE THAT IS LONG
OVERDUE. YOUR EYES TELL A STORY OF SUCH A HEARTBREAKING
TALE. SORTED CHAPTERS OF BOTH REGRET AND HEARTLESS
BETRAYAL. I SEE THE SEARCHING AND THE HOPE THAT FLICKERS
LIKE A CANDLE BARELY BURNING. I SEE THE TEARS BEING HELD
BACK AS YOU STAY QUIET WHILE SILENTLY YEARNING."

STEPHEN D. RHOADES
(S.D.R.)
SHAKESPEARE'S RAVEN 2

Photo: Riya Albert / Jewelry: Wonderland MC

"She has held me without touching my skin. She is my kryptonite and my favorite sin. She makes this dark soul smile at a mere thought of her. She alone had the power to make this heart of stone stir. She has the ability to make me feel strong when I am in fact weak. Her arms are the home I truly seek. In her beauty I sit and bask. To remain within her presence forever is all I ask.

Stephen D. Rhoades

(S.D.R.)

Shakespeare's Raven 2

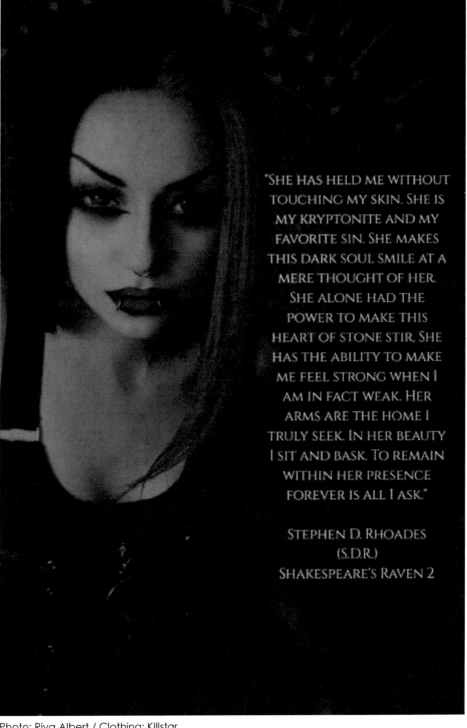

"SHE HAS HELD ME WITHOUT TOUCHING MY SKIN. SHE IS MY KRYPTONITE AND MY FAVORITE SIN. SHE MAKES THIS DARK SOUL SMILE AT A MERE THOUGHT OF HER. SHE ALONE HAD THE POWER TO MAKE THIS HEART OF STONE STIR. SHE HAS THE ABILITY TO MAKE ME FEEL STRONG WHEN I AM IN FACT WEAK. HER ARMS ARE THE HOME I TRULY SEEK. IN HER BEAUTY I SIT AND BASK. TO REMAIN WITHIN HER PRESENCE FOREVER IS ALL I ASK."

STEPHEN D. RHOADES
(S.D.R.)
SHAKESPEARE'S RAVEN 2

Photo: Riya Albert / Clothing: Kıllstar

"I see your fire despite the rain.

I sense the confusion in your pain.

I hear the whispers of the words you cannot express.

I see the beauty in the mess."

Stephen D. Rhoades

(S.D.R.)

Shakespeare's Raven 2

"I SEE YOUR FIRE DESPITE THE RAIN.
I SENSE THE CONFUSION IN YOUR PAIN.
I HEAR THE WHISPERS OF THE WORDS
YOU CAN'T EXPRESS.
I SEE THE BEAUTY IN THE MESS."

STEPHEN D. RHOADES
(S.D.R.)
SHAKESPEARE'S RAVEN 2

Photo: Riya Albert

"She needed to be loved in a way that made her broken pieces feel whole. So I gently held her heart as I entangled myself in her soul"

Stephen D. Rhoades

(S.D.R.)

Shakespeare's Raven 2

"SHE NEEDED TO BE LOVED IN A WAY THAT MADE HER BROKEN PIECES FEEL WHOLE. SO I GENTLY HELD HER HEART AS I ENTANGLED MYSELF IN HER SOUL"

STEPHEN D. RHOADES
(S.D.R.)
SHAKESPEARE'S RAVEN 2

Photo: Riya Albert / Clothing: Killstar

Beautiful, what I want first and foremost is your heart, and your mind. I desire what no one else has taken the time to find.

Then I will show you what a masterpiece you are. We will celebrate the beauty within every scar.

You will see what I see and come to know your incredible worth.

Because you are proof that angel's do indeed walk upon the Earth.

Understood?

Stephen D. Rhoades

(S.D.R.)

Shakespeare's Raven 2

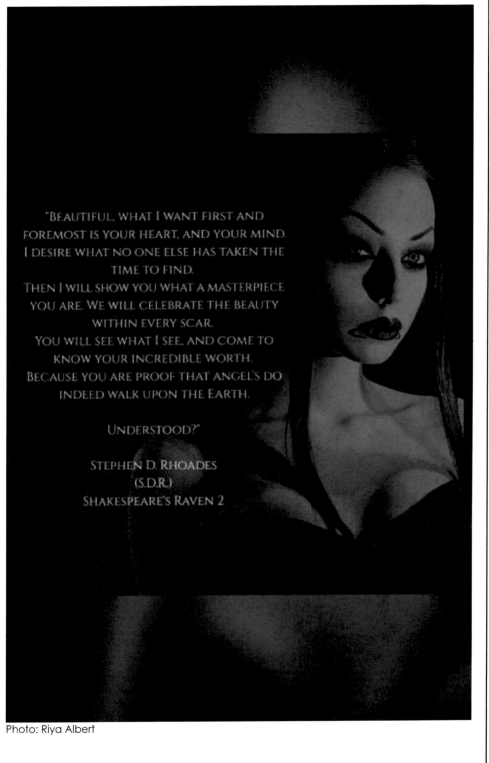

"BEAUTIFUL, WHAT I WANT FIRST AND
FOREMOST IS YOUR HEART, AND YOUR MIND.
I DESIRE WHAT NO ONE ELSE HAS TAKEN THE
TIME TO FIND.
THEN I WILL SHOW YOU WHAT A MASTERPIECE
YOU ARE. WE WILL CELEBRATE THE BEAUTY
WITHIN EVERY SCAR.
YOU WILL SEE WHAT I SEE, AND COME TO
KNOW YOUR INCREDIBLE WORTH.
BECAUSE YOU ARE PROOF THAT ANGEL'S DO
INDEED WALK UPON THE EARTH.

UNDERSTOOD?"

STEPHEN D. RHOADES
(S.D.R.)
SHAKESPEARE'S RAVEN 2

Photo: Riya Albert

"The world often cannot see past the beauty of my skin. They easily forget the living soul that lives within. Appreciate my beauty, but do not forget I deserve, and need, respect, and love too. Though I have been tested and scarred by various acts of betrayal, inside me there is still a little girl that has hope placed in what many would call a fairytale. So love me not in careless words often spoken but love me in ways that values what is unseen as well as broken."

Stephen D. Rhoades

(S.D.R.)

Shakespeare's Raven 2

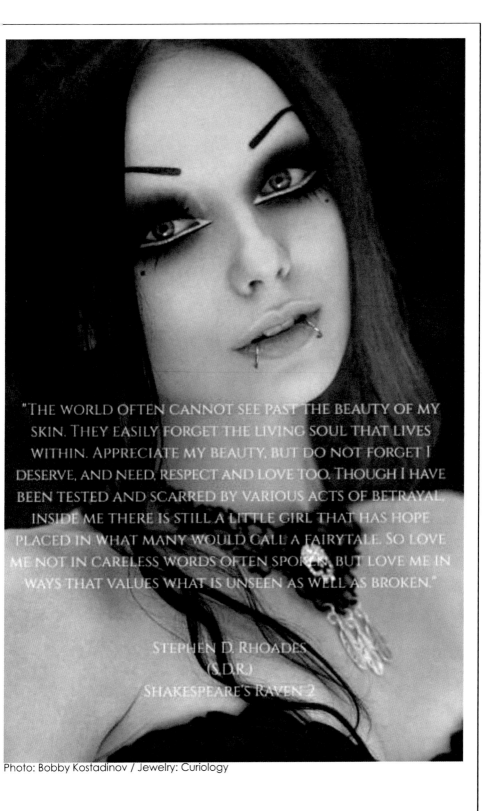

"THE WORLD OFTEN CANNOT SEE PAST THE BEAUTY OF MY
SKIN. THEY EASILY FORGET THE LIVING SOUL THAT LIVES
WITHIN. APPRECIATE MY BEAUTY, BUT DO NOT FORGET I
DESERVE, AND NEED, RESPECT AND LOVE TOO. THOUGH I HAVE
BEEN TESTED AND SCARRED BY VARIOUS ACTS OF BETRAYAL,
INSIDE ME THERE IS STILL A LITTLE GIRL THAT HAS HOPE
PLACED IN WHAT MANY WOULD CALL A FAIRYTALE. SO LOVE
ME NOT IN CARELESS WORDS OFTEN SPOKEN, BUT LOVE ME IN
WAYS THAT VALUES WHAT IS UNSEEN AS WELL AS BROKEN."

STEPHEN D. RHOADES
(S.D.R.)
SHAKESPEARE'S RAVEN 2

Photo: Bobby Kostadinov / Jewelry: Curiology

"She is the essence of my biggest temptation, and favorite sin. She embodies every desire I feel within.

Beautiful darkness has a heartbeat, and the heartbeat belongs to her. A sweet tasting poison with no known cure."

Stephen D. Rhoades

(S.D.R.)

Shakespeare's Raven 2

"SHE IS THE ESSENCE OF MY BIGGEST TEMPTATION AND FAVORITE SIN. SHE EMBODIES EVERY DESIRE I FEEL WITHIN.

BEAUTIFUL DARKNESS HAS A HEARTBEAT, AND THE HEARTBEAT BELONGS TO HER. A SWEET-TASTING POISON WITH NO KNOWN CURE.."

STEPHEN D. RHOADES
(S.D.R.)
SHAKESPEARE'S RAVEN 2

"Here is what's going to happen.

I am going to love the hell out of you regardless of how hard it might be.

I am going to tear down the walls you built and replace them with my arms.

I will love the parts of you that you may hate and show you the beauty in them.

Understood?"

Stephen D. Rhoades

(S.D.R.)

Shakespeare's Raven 2

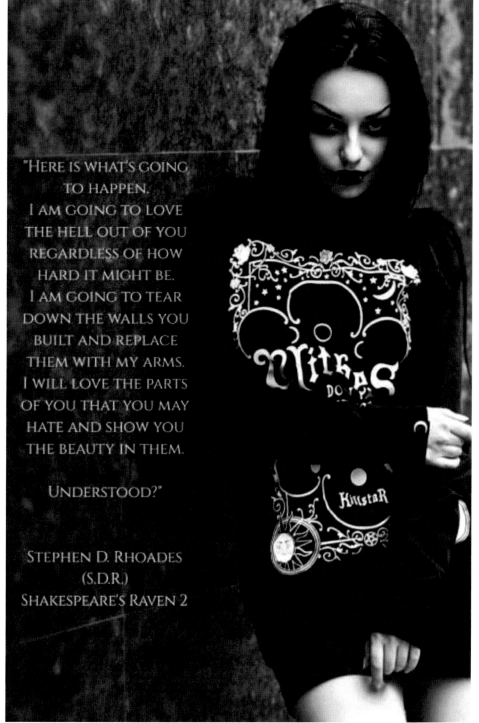

"HERE IS WHAT'S GOING
TO HAPPEN.
I AM GOING TO LOVE
THE HELL OUT OF YOU
REGARDLESS OF HOW
HARD IT MIGHT BE.
I AM GOING TO TEAR
DOWN THE WALLS YOU
BUILT AND REPLACE
THEM WITH MY ARMS.
I WILL LOVE THE PARTS
OF YOU THAT YOU MAY
HATE AND SHOW YOU
THE BEAUTY IN THEM.

UNDERSTOOD?"

STEPHEN D. RHOADES
(S.D.R.)
SHAKESPEARE'S RAVEN 2

Photo by: Bobby Kostadinov   Clothing: Killstar

Stephen Rhoades is an Author, Poet, and Van Lifer who lives in the Pacific Northwest along the Oregon Coast. If you enjoyed this book, please check out his other books that are available on Amazon and check out his Facebook page "Shakespeare's Raven" and Shakespeare's Raven 2".

Made in the USA
Las Vegas, NV
13 October 2023

78975068R00038